Wilma's mum had a sister called Joy. Joy and Ben had a baby. He was a little boy called Troy.

Wilf and Wilma liked the baby.
"He's a good little boy," said Wilf.

"He's a bundle of joy," said Ben, "but he has a loud voice when he cries."

Troy woke up. But he didn’t cry.
“Let me tickle his tum,” said Wilf.
Troy began to giggle and chuckle.

Wilma wanted to cuddle him.
“He likes to wriggle,” she said.

Then there was a loud noise.
"What was that noise?" said Joy.

"It sounds like water," said Mum.

Oh no! A pipe had broken. It had broken in the middle. There was a big spout of water.

Water gushed into the room.
It made a big puddle.

The puddle grew bigger and bigger.
“My feet are wet,” said Joy.

At last Ben fixed the pipe.
Troy began to cry. So did Joy.

“The carpet is spoiled,” said Joy.
“It will all dry out,” said Dad,
“but it will take time.”

"Come back to our house," said Mum.
"You don't have a choice."

So they all went back to Wilf and Wilma's house.

Troy began to cry.
"He has got a loud voice," said Dad.

Wilf gave Troy a rattle. Wilma found a little bell. It went tinkle, tinkle, tinkle.

"He needs to be back at home,"
said Joy.

Wilf held Troy, and Wilma sang a song to him.

"Wilma has a nice voice," said Joy.
"Troy is enjoying it."

Troy woke up in the night.

Joy and Ben woke up.

Waaaa!

Mum and Dad woke up.

Waaaa!

Wilf and Wilma woke up.

Waaaa!

Wilma sang to Troy again.
“Boil the kettle, Dad,” said Mum,
“and make a cup of tea.”

"He's settled down," said Wilf. "He's gone to sleep."

Oh no!
So have the
grown-ups!